W9-BIM-175

616.4
TIG

Tiger, Steven.

Diabetes.

33197000042486

$11.98

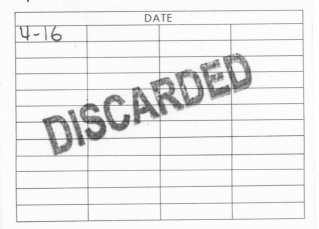

DATE		
4-16		

DISCARDED

BAKER & TAYLOR BOOKS

UNDERSTANDING DISEASE

DIABETES

UNDERSTANDING DISEASE

ARTHRITIS
THE COMMON COLD AND INFLUENZA
DIABETES
HEART DISEASE

UNDERSTANDING DISEASE

DIABETES

STEVEN TIGER

ILLUSTRATED BY MICHAEL REINGOLD

MEDICAL CONSULTANT: JOHN F. NICHOLSON, M.D.

DIRECTOR, CHILDREN'S DIABETIC SERVICE
COLUMBIA-PRESBYTERIAN COLLEGE OF PHYSICIANS AND SURGEONS, NEW YORK CITY

JULIAN MESSNER
A Division of Simon & Schuster, Inc., New York

Text copyright © 1987 by Steven Tiger
Illustrations © 1987 by Michael Reingold
All rights reserved including the right of reproduction in whole or in part in any
form. Published by Julian Messner, A Division of Simon & Schuster, Inc. Simon
& Schuster Building, Rockefeller Center, 1230 Avenue of the Americas, New York,
New York 10020.

JULIAN MESSNER and colophon are trademarks of Simon & Schuster, Inc.
Manufactured in the United States of America

10   9   8   7   6   5   4   3

Library of Congress Cataloguing in Publication Data
Tiger, Steven.   Diabetes.
    (Understanding disease)
    Includes index.
    Summary: Discusses how the body uses foods, food groups, what goes
wrong when diabetes occurs, the different types of diabetes, treatment,
and research for future improvements in treatment and prevention.
    1. Diabetes – Juvenile literature.   [1. Diabetes]   I. Title.   II. Series.
RC660.5.T54   1987   616.4′62   86-23498
ISBN 0-671-63273-6

CONTENTS

 # 1: WHAT IS DIABETES?

Diabetes is not a single disease. Several different diseases are called diabetes. What do they have in common? In each case, the body cannot handle a certain type of sugar normally. Diabetes can have different causes, and it can have many different effects on the body. But at the center of all these conditions is a problem with sugar.

The full name for this group of diseases is diabetes mellitus.

Diabetes is from a Greek word that means "drain" – people with diabetes lose a lot of water from their bodies. *Mellitus* means "honey" or "sweet" – the blood and other body fluids often hold a load of extra sugar.

Many people think that diabetes just means having too much sugar in the blood. That is not correct. Diabetics (patients with diabetes) often do have too much sugar in the blood – but they can also have too little sugar, which may be even more dangerous. And it is not just sugar. The body's way of handling fats and proteins is also disturbed.

WHO GETS DIABETES?

Diabetes is a common disease. Over twelve million Americans – about one out of every twenty people – have some form of diabetes, and only half of them know it. Anyone can get diabetes – men and women, children and adults, and people from many different races. But certain groups are more likely than others to get specific types of diabetes.

In some other countries, diabetes is less common. As we will see, the most common type of diabetes occurs in people who are obese (overweight). In advanced industrial nations like the United States, obesity is common and so is this type of diabetes. In countries where obesity is rare, diabetes is unusual.

HOW SERIOUS IS DIABETES?

Among diseases (not accidents and injuries), diabetes and the problems it causes are the third leading cause of death in the United States. Diabetes is the main cause of blindness in adults. People with diabetes are more likely than others to have kidney disease or heart disease. Diabetes can damage the blood vessels, which decreases the amount of oxygen that can reach the legs and feet. In severe cases, these areas can actually die from lack of oxygen, and then they must be removed by surgery. About forty thousand such operations must be done each year in this country because of diabetes.

Every year, more than 2 million people have to go into the hospital because of problems related to diabetes. For patients, the cost of diabetes is a higher risk of sickness and death. For our nation, the cost is eighteen billion dollars each year for

Anyone may get diabetes. About twelve million Americans – one out of every twenty people – have diabetes, and only half of them know it.

medical care and time lost from work.

CAN ANYTHING BE DONE?

Right now, there is no cure for diabetes. But it usually can be controlled. There has been some progress made in treating this serious disease, but the best news is that the most common type of diabetes can often be prevented altogether.

In the next chapter, we will see how the body normally handles sugar and other substances in food. Then we will be able to understand what goes wrong in diabetes.

2: FOOD AND METABOLISM

THE FOODS WE EAT

All the foods we eat – bread and cereals, dairy products, fruits and vegetables, meat and fish – contain three main types of nutrients: carbohydrates*, proteins*, and fats. Different foods contain different amounts of these nutrients. Fruits, vegetables, and grains, for example, have a lot of carbohydrate, some protein, and

*Defined in the Glossary.

very little fat. Dairy products and meats have a lot of protein and fat, but less carbohydrate.

Foods also contain small amounts of complex substances called vitamins, which are needed for many of the processes that build and protect the body. Certain mineral elements are also needed, such as iron for making red blood cells, and calcium for making the bones hard and for controlling how the muscles contract. Each vitamin and mineral does something special, so if even one of them is missing, the body cannot work properly. But a good, balanced diet contains all the required vitamins and minerals.

Now let's look at the three main nutrients.

Carbohydrates consist of sugars and starches. All carbohydrates are made of units called saccharides*. Sugars are made of just one or two units, so they are called monosaccharides or disaccharides. Starches are built up of longer chains, so they are called polysaccharides. The sugar that we keep on the kitchen table is called sucrose, but there are many other sugars, such as lactose (found in milk) and fructose (found in honey and many fruits). Foods like bread, potatoes, and spaghetti contain a lot of starch; liver also has a good amount of starch, but most other meats, poultry, and fish have very little starch.

Proteins are long chains of compounds called amino acids*. There are twenty-one different amino acids, and dozens or even hundreds of them may be linked together to form different proteins. The order in which they are linked determines what kind of protein they make up. Of the twenty-one amino acids, ten are called "essential," because the human body cannot make them, and we must get them from our food. The body can manufacture all the other amino acids from simpler substances. Proteins that come from animals (meat, fish, eggs, and milk) are "complete," because they contain all ten essential amino acids. Proteins from plants (such as nuts, beans, and cereal grains) are "incomplete," because they lack one or more of the essential amino acids. However, when certain kinds of plant proteins are put together, the combination is complete, because each plant protein supplies the essential amino acids missing from the other.

Fats consist of three long chains of fatty acids* linked to a glycerol* molecule, forming a structure called a triglyceride*. These are the actual fats found in animal flesh and milk. Whole milk and cream, butter, cheeses, and ice cream all contain butterfat from cow's milk. All meats contain fat; some meats, like bacon, are very fatty. Oils found in certain plants, such as nuts and seeds, can supply what the body needs just as well as animal fat can. Margarine is a food product made from plant oils.

WHAT WE GET FROM FOODS

The body uses food as a source of energy and to build new tissues. Carbohydrates are the main source of fuel for energy. But when we work or exercise, the body's supply of carbohydrates goes down. As that happens, the body starts using stored fat for fuel.

Proteins are the "building blocks" for new tissues. Different kinds of proteins, made of different combinations of amino acids, are needed to build new muscle, skin, blood cells – in fact, almost everything in the body.

A certain amount of fat must be stored around the body in adipose* cells – special cells that are designed to store fat. Fat helps to cushion vital organs like the kidneys, and it helps to keep the body warm. Fats are also used to form many compounds that the body needs, and it is the body's main fuel as soon as the carbohydrate supply goes down.

HOW WE ABSORB NUTRIENTS

When we eat, food enters the stomach and then goes into the intestine. The nutrients in the food must be broken down into the tiniest particles so that they can be absorbed from the intestine. From the intestine, nutrients are carried by the

12

bloodstream to the liver and the rest of the body, supplying energy and building materials to all the cells. There are special systems for absorbing and using each of the different nutrients. All together, these systems are called metabolism*.

CARBOHYDRATE METABOLISM

Carbohydrates must be broken down into monosaccharide units. An enzyme* in saliva starts the process. Other enzymes, in the intestine, finish the job and help the monosaccharides pass through the intestinal wall, into the bloodstream. The monosaccharides are carried to the liver, where a great number of chemical processes take place.

Many of the processes in the liver involve a monosaccharide called glucose*, which is the body's best fuel. In the liver, some of the glucose is converted into a storage form called glycogen*, which can be quickly converted back to glucose whenever it is needed. In the liver and in adipose cells, extra glucose is converted to glycerol, which then combines with fatty acids to form triglyceride – that is, human fat for storage. A hormone* called insulin* promotes these processes. In fact, insulin plays a vital role in many metabolic processes.

METABOLISM OF PROTEINS AND FATS

Proteins must also be broken down into their units, the amino acids. That is done by stomach acid and enzymes from the stomach, pancreas*, and intestine. The amino acids are absorbed through the intestine and carried to the liver and the rest of the body. They may be used to build new proteins for the body – another process promoted by insulin (along with another hormone, called growth hormone). When there

13

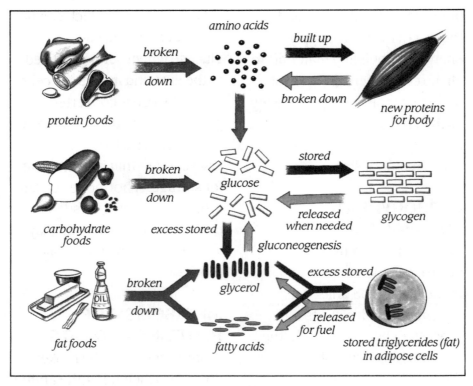

Glucose is at the center of all the metabolic processes.

is an excess of free amino acids, the liver converts some of them to glucose or to fat.

Fats are also broken down. An enzyme from the pancreas enters the intestine and splits the long chains of fatty acids away from the glycerol. The chains are then broken into shorter chains. Fats absorbed from the intestine go through special channels that carry them to the blood circulation system. The blood will finally take them to the liver and the rest of the body.

In the liver, glycerol is converted into glucose or glycogen. Some fatty acids in the blood are used as fuel by the muscles. But if there is an excess of glycerol and fatty acids, they will be combined together again to form new triglycerides for storage in the adipose cells. Similarly, excess glucose enters the adipose cells and is converted to glycerol, which then combines with fatty acids to form triglycerides. Again we see the importance of insulin – for insulin pushes fatty acids from the bloodstream into the adipose cells, while growth hormone moves stored fat back into circulation.

GETTING ENERGY FROM FOOD

The best fuel for most cells – especially in the brain – is glucose. Carbohydrate foods bring in a load of glucose, but most of it gets stored as glycogen or fat. Glycogen is stored in the liver and muscles, ready to be changed back into glucose. But the body can't store very much glycogen, so most of the energy for cells must come from stored fat.

While we work and play, glucose in the blood will supply the energy – but only as long as there is still enough glycogen left to keep replacing it. Within a few hours after eating, the glycogen supply is down, and the glucose level starts falling. Then the body starts releasing and breaking down stored fat. As triglycerides are broken down, the glycerol is converted back to glucose for use as fuel for the brain, while the fatty acids are used as fuel by the muscles and other parts of the body.

CHANGING ONE SUBSTANCE INTO ANOTHER

As we see, the liver produces some amazing changes in the nutrients we absorb from food. Some of the glucose from carbohydrate foods is converted to glycogen, which can be changed right back whenever more glucose is needed. When the liver and the muscles have all the glycogen they can hold, additional glucose is converted to glycerol, which then combines with fatty acids to form triglycerides for storage. When stored fat is broken down, the glycerol is converted back to glucose, while the fatty acids are used for fuel. Some of the fatty acids are converted by the liver into chemicals called ketones*, which are also used as fuel. Fats from food are broken down and put together again as human fat for storage. Amino acids from protein foods can be built up into human proteins or converted to glucose or fat.

Did you notice that *any* type of nutrient can be changed into glucose in the liver? Carbohydrate foods are broken down to their glucose units. But both glycerol from fat and certain amino acids from protein can be converted into glucose. In fact, this process is called gluconeogenesis* – "making new glucose."

THE ROLE OF INSULIN

The pancreas makes enzymes that enter the intestine to help break down different nutrients. But inside the pancreas, there are special areas that produce hormones. These areas are like tiny islands surrounded by the rest of the pancreas tissue. They are called the Islets of Langerhans* (named for the scientist who found them). The Islets have different kinds of cells, including alpha-cells, which produce a hormone called glucagon*, and beta-cells, which produce insulin.

These two hormones act in opposite ways. Glucagon raises the level of glucose in the blood by helping to convert glycogen back into glucose and by promoting gluconeogenesis. Insulin lowers the level of glucose in the blood by helping to convert glucose into glycogen, by slowing down gluconeogenesis, and by moving glucose from the blood into the

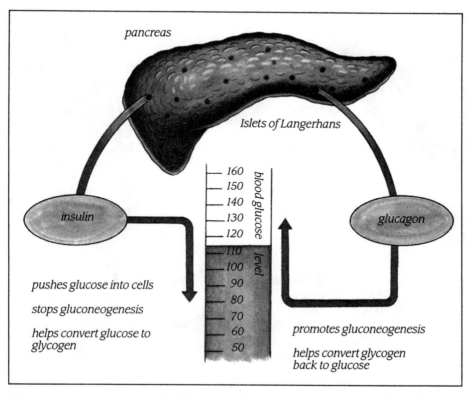

pancreas

Islets of Langerhans

blood glucose level

insulin

glucagon

160
150
140
130
120
110
100
90
80
70
60
50

pushes glucose into cells

stops gluconeogenesis

helps convert glucose to glycogen

promotes gluconeogenesis

helps convert glycogen back to glucose

Blood glucose level is held steady by the hormones from the pancreas. Insulin lowers the glucose level, glucagon raises the level.

cells for use as fuel. (Cells in the brain and a few other parts of the body can take in glucose without the aid of insulin, but most cells need insulin to take in glucose.) Insulin also promotes the production of new protein from amino acids, and the production and storage of fat in adipose cells.

With these two hormones balancing each other, the body keeps the glucose level steady. Exercise uses up lots of fuel, so the glucose levels start to fall. But as that happens, the

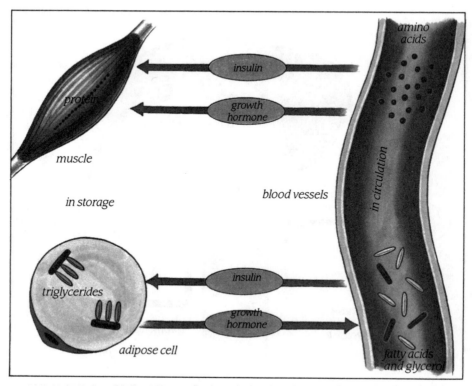

Insulin and growth hormone both promote the building of protein in muscle, from amino acids. But these hormones act in opposite ways on fat. Insulin promotes the building of triglycerides from fatty acids and glycerol in circulation, for storage in adipose cells. Growth hormone promotes the breakdown of stored fat, releasing fatty acids and glycerol into circulation.

pancreas produces a little less insulin and a little more glucagon, and the glucose level rises back to normal. Eating raises the level of glucose in the blood. But as that happens, more insulin and less glucagon are produced, and the glucose level falls back to normal. In fact, the level of glucose in the bloodstream is adjusted every moment, to keep it as steady and as close to the normal amount as possible.

Now we have learned that insulin allows glucose to enter the cells, helps excess glucose to be stored as glycogen or fat, and promotes tissue growth with new proteins. In diabetes, there are problems with insulin and the processes that depend on insulin. In the next chapters, we will see what happens to these metabolic processes in people who have diabetes.

3: TYPE I DIABETES MELLITUS

People who have Type I diabetes are unable to produce their own insulin, so they have to take injections of insulin. That is why this condition is also called "insulin-dependent diabetes mellitus." Only a small portion of all the people with diabetes have Type I diabetes, but they often have the most severe disease.

Type I diabetes often runs in families. Close relatives of a person with this condition are more likely than other people to have problems with glucose metabolism. That doesn't mean that a child will get diabetes just because one or both parents have diabetes. But that child is more likely to develop diabetes than the child of two non-diabetic parents.

Most cases of Type I diabetes are found in children and young adults. In fact, this condition was once called "juvenile-onset diabetes." However, that name is no longer used, since the disease can occur at any age. Almost all cases of diabetes that occur before the age of twenty years are Type I. As people get older, Type I diabetes occurs less often, and Type II diabetes (see Chapter Four) becomes more common. But new cases of Type I disease have been found even in people over eighty years old.

NO INSULIN IS PRODUCED

The beta-cells in the Islets of Langerhans in the pancreas make insulin. In Type I diabetes, these beta-cells are destroyed. No one knows exactly how or why this happens, but one idea is that certain viruses can attack the beta-cells. Another idea is that the body's own immune system – which guards against infection by fighting off viruses and germs – makes a mistake and attacks the beta-cells as if they did not belong in the body.

As the beta-cells are destroyed, the body produces less and less insulin, and the symptoms of diabetes get worse and worse. Finally, there is no insulin produced at all.

WHEN THERE IS NO INSULIN

We know that insulin allows glucose to enter the cells. Without insulin, the cells do not get the glucose they need for fuel, and the glucose just piles up in the blood and the fluids outside the cells, unable to get in. As the level of glucose in the blood rises, the cells use fatty acids for fuel. Now remember that another action of insulin is to promote the storage of fat, and that growth hormone works in the opposite way, releasing fat from storage. When there is no insulin, the action of growth hormone takes over, and fat comes out of storage. The fat is broken down, releasing fatty acids at exactly the time when the cells – which can't take in glucose without insulin – need fatty acids for fuel!

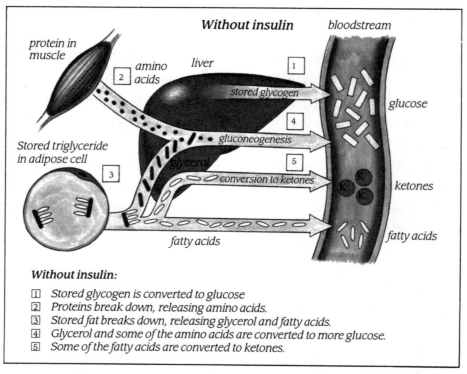

Without insulin

bloodstream

protein in muscle

amino acids

liver

[2]

[1]

stored glycogen

glucose

Stored triglyceride in adipose cell

[3]

glycerol

[4]

gluconeogenesis

[5]

conversion to ketones

ketones

fatty acids

fatty acids

Without insulin:

1. Stored glycogen is converted to glucose
2. Proteins break down, releasing amino acids.
3. Stored fat breaks down, releasing glycerol and fatty acids.
4. Glycerol and some of the amino acids are converted to more glucose.
5. Some of the fatty acids are converted to ketones.

Glucose, put out by the liver and unable to get into the cells without insulin, builds up in the blood. The breakdown of fat is so fast that ketones build up faster than they can be used as fuel, causing acidosis.

Ketones, made from fatty acids by the liver, can also be used for fuel. However, ketones are harmful if they build up in the body. Under normal conditions, ketones are produced slowly and used up as soon as they appear. But without insulin, so much fatty acid is released from stored fat that the liver produces ketones much faster than they can be used up. As they pile up in the body's fluids, they create a serious condition called acidosis*, which means that the amount of acid in the body's fluids goes way above normal.

Think of having a salad. A little vinegar in the salad dressing is fine, but a whole bottle of vinegar would ruin the food. Similarly, too much acid upsets all the chemical balances in the body.

GLUCOSE BUILDS UP

But the problems in Type I diabetes don't stop there. As stored fat is released and broken down, a load of glycerol also enters the circulation. When it reaches the liver, the glycerol is converted to glucose – and there is already too much glucose in the blood because it can't get into the cells! The lack of insulin also causes body proteins to break down, releasing amino acids. Some of those amino acids, along with fatty acids and ketones, can be used for fuel – and some are converted by the liver into still more glucose! Normally, all this extra glucose would be converted to glycogen and fat for storage – but that process does require insulin.

Having so much glucose in the blood creates more problems. Water is naturally attracted toward substances like glucose and salt. When there is more glucose in the blood and other body fluids, more water will be attracted toward it. Then, as blood is filtered through the kidneys, a load of glucose spills out into the urine, and a large amount of water comes out along with it. That is why people with diabetes lose water, and why they must drink a lot of water to replace what they lose in the urine. Some people, especially elderly people, don't drink enough water. Then they can become dehydrated*. If that happens, their kidneys cannot work properly, and that can also lead to acidosis, since it is the kidneys' job to get rid of extra acids before they can build up in the body.

The cause of all these problems is the lack of insulin. Taking insulin can prevent many of

23

these problems, but it does not cure the disease.

EFFECTS ON THE BODY

Normally, the pancreas releases insulin and glucagon exactly as needed to keep the glucose level steady. Since people who have Type I diabetes can't make their own insulin, they must take it by injection. However, taking insulin injections a few times during the day cannot hold the glucose level as steady as when the pancreas releases insulin moment by moment, as it is needed. Many diabetics have glucose levels that are always above normal. But the level of glucose in the blood can also be too low, if the person takes too much insulin or too little food.

People with diabetes tend to have more physical problems during their lives than other people. Most of these problems are caused by damage to blood vessels. Doctors are not sure what causes this damage. But many experts think it happens mainly when the diabetes is not controlled by treatment. If that is so, then vessel damage can be prevented by keeping the disease under control. That means holding the glucose level as steady and as close to normal as possible. It is not always easy to control diabetes, especially Type I, but it can be done.

DAMAGE TO LARGE BLOOD VESSELS

Uncontrolled diabetes damages both large and small blood vessels. Fatty deposits slowly plug up large vessels. The heart has to work harder to pump blood past the deposits. Calcium hardens these deposits, making the vessels rigid. That can raise the blood pressure, which also makes the heart work harder. After a while, the heart can become "worn out." If a clot of blood forms at a deposit, it can travel further down along the vessel, causing great damage wherever it finally gets stuck. A blood clot that reaches the brain can cause a *stroke*, which can kill or paralyze a person. If a blood vessel becomes completely blocked by the hardened deposit, the areas of the body that are normally supplied with blood from that vessel cannot receive the oxygen and nutrients they need, and the cells will die.

This type of vessel damage is called atherosclerosis*, which means "fatty deposits, with hardening." Atherosclerosis in the arteries of the heart can cause chest pain or even a heart attack (an area of the heart that dies from lack of oxygen). Atherosclerosis can occur whether or not a person has diabetes. But it tends to occur at an earlier age in those with diabetes.

Blockage of blood vessels in the feet is a special problem for diabetics. Blood circulation to the feet is usually not as good as circulation to other parts of the body, even in people who do not have diabetes. Then if atherosclerosis reduces the amount of blood that can get through the vessels, the feet may be affected sooner and more severely than other areas of the body. When tissues die from lack of blood, it is called gangrene*. These dead areas must be removed by surgery. Diabetes is the most common cause of gangrene in the feet, and that is the most common reason for this type of operation.

DAMAGE TO SMALL BLOOD VESSELS

Atherosclerosis in larger blood vessels, as we just learned, can happen whether or not a person has diabetes. But diabetics can also suffer a special kind of damage to small blood vessels. The very smallest vessels – the capillaries – are surrounded by a thin membrane. Diabetes can cause this membrane to become thicker. That makes it harder for oxygen and nutrients to pass through the capillaries to reach the cells.

25

This type of damage to the small vessels can cause serious problems wherever it occurs, especially in the eye, the kidney, and the heart. It can also harm the nerve cells, causing a loss of feeling in different parts of the body. When there is nerve damage as well as vessel damage in the feet, the problems are multiplied. Because of the loss of feeling, the person cannot feel pain from injuries or heavy pressure on the bottom of the foot. Large open sores can develop, which can become badly infected. Germs grow quickly where there is a high level of glucose in the fluids. Also, the vessel damage reduces the amount of blood reaching the infected area, so that white blood cells – which work to clean up infections – can't get to where they are needed.

Doctors and scientists are not sure what causes this type of damage to the tiny blood vessels. But most experts think that it is caused by the metabolic effects of diabetes, especially the high levels of glucose in the blood. That is why treatment to control the amount of glucose is so important.

Next, we'll learn about Type II diabetes, similar to Type I in some ways and very different in other ways.

4: TYPE II DIABETES MELLITUS

Type II diabetes mellitus is by far the most common form of diabetes in the United States. Almost 90 percent of all the cases of diabetes that occur in this country are Type II. It is almost never found in children, but it is more and more common as people get older. That is the opposite of Type I diabetes, which usually develops when people are young and rarely strikes older people. Type II diabetes was once called "adult-onset diabetes," but that name is no longer used since it has been found – rarely – in people who are only about twenty years old. Most people are over forty years old when Type I diabetes is found. And about three-fourths of them are obese (seriously overweight).

Like Type I diabetes, Type II disease often runs in families, so that close relatives of a person with Type II diabetes are more likely to get the disease than members of a family where no one has any kind of diabetes.

THE DIFFERENCES IN THE TWO TYPES

Type I diabetes occurs just as often in boys and young men as in girls and young women, and there is no clear difference in how often it occurs in white people and in black people. But Type II diabetes is more common in older blacks, especially black women. This disease is also common among certain American Indian tribes, but very rare among the Innuit (Eskimos) and Asian people. No one knows why these racial patterns occur.

The main difference between Type I and Type II diabetes is that Type I is "insulin-dependent" and Type II is "non-insulin-dependent." In other words, people with Type I diabetes cannot make their own insulin, so they must take it by injection. People with Type II diabetes have a different problem: they can make at least some insulin, but the insulin does not do what it is supposed to do. Most people with Type II diabetes do not have to take injections of insulin. Instead, they have to help their own insulin do its job.

PROBLEMS WITH INSULIN

People with Type II diabetes produce some insulin, but less than normal. It may take them much longer to produce and release insulin after a meal. And what they produce may not do its job.

One of the main jobs of insulin is to help glucose get inside cells. To do that, the insulin molecule has to attach itself to a receptor*, a special area on the surface of the cell. Once it is attached, a whole series of events takes place inside the cell to allow glucose to enter. Doctors and scientists are not sure what goes wrong in Type II diabetes. Some experts think that the receptors do not let insulin become attached. Others believe that a large

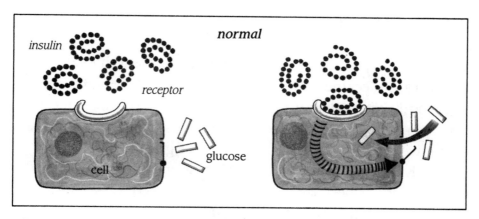

Glucose can't enter the cell until insulin attaches to a receptor. That starts a process inside the cell to let glucose in.

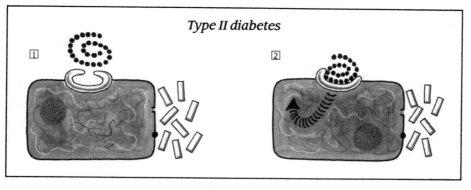

In Type II diabetes, there is less insulin and it doesn't work well: (1) The insulin can't attach to the receptor, or (2) The process inside the cell goes wrong. As a result glucose is unable to enter the cell.

number of receptors are lost completely from the cell surfaces, leaving very few places for insulin molecules to attach themselves. The newest idea is that something goes wrong inside the cell after insulin attaches to the receptor. Or it may be a combination of problems.

THE IMPORTANCE OF DIET

As we have learned, a person's age and race affect the chance of getting diabetes. While we cannot do anything about those factors, we can certainly try to keep body weight normal. That is very important, because obesity is the main factor that makes people more likely to get Type II diabetes. Therefore, controlling body weight is the most important thing we can do to prevent it. And as we'll see in Chapter Seven, weight control is also very important in treating the disease. In fact, many people with Type II diabetes can keep it under control just by eating properly.

Doctors aren't sure why obesity leads to diabetes in some people. It might be because most overweight people eat too much food that is loaded with fat and sugar, and that causes the insulin-producing beta-cells in the Islets of Langerhans to be overworked.

When we eat starchy food, it takes time to break the starches down to monosaccharide units. Therefore, glucose is absorbed gradually from the intestine into the bloodstream. Insulin can be released gradually to help the glucose enter the cells and to promote the conversion of glucose to glycerol (for making fat) or glycogen for storage. But when we eat sugary food, the sugar is ready to be absorbed almost at once, so a tremendous amount of glucose enters the bloodstream very quickly – and the pancreas has to produce a tremendous amount of insulin very quickly to deal with it. The same thing happens with food that contains a lot of fat: the pancreas must quickly make a lot of insulin to get the absorbed glycerol and fatty acids out of the blood and into storage cells.

FAT, SUGAR, AND INSULIN

In people who are born with a tendency to have problems with producing insulin, this kind of diet, high in fat and sugar, can exhaust the beta-cells, so that they can no longer make insulin fast enough to control blood glucose levels. Then the body cells or their insulin receptors may be affected by the high glucose levels, so that insulin doesn't work even when it is produced.

That may explain why Type II diabetes usually appears in older people – it takes years for the beta-cells to become "worn out" from overwork. And that may also be why diet is so important during treatment – by avoiding foods that contain big loads of fat and sugar, we give the pancreas time to produce enough insulin to keep blood glucose levels under control.

EFFECTS ON THE BODY

Whatever the cause of Type II diabetes, the result is hyperglycemia* – high levels of glucose in the blood. Most of the problems that occur in people with Type I diabetes can also occur in people with Type II disease. They can develop atherosclerosis in the larger blood vessels and thickening of the membrane in the smallest vessels. And they can develop all the conditions that are caused by damage to the blood vessels: blindness, kidney failure, heart disease, nerve damage, and serious problems in the feet, including infections and gangrene.

One problem that rarely happens in people with Type II diabetes is acidosis. In Chapter Three, we learned that when there is absolutely no insulin, a large amount of stored fat is released and broken down. Some of the fatty acids are converted by the liver into ketones, which can also be used as a fuel. But the ketones are formed so fast that they pile up in the body, causing acidosis. Experts believe that even the small amount of insulin produced in people with Type II diabetes is enough to control the release and

31

breakdown of stored fat, so that ketones do not pile up too fast. But it takes much more insulin to get glucose into the cells so that blood glucose levels do not rise. That is why people with Type II diabetes often develop hyperglycemia, but not acidosis.

Almost all cases of diabetes are either Type I or Type II. But a small number of people have other kinds of diabetes, and those conditions are the topic of the next chapter.

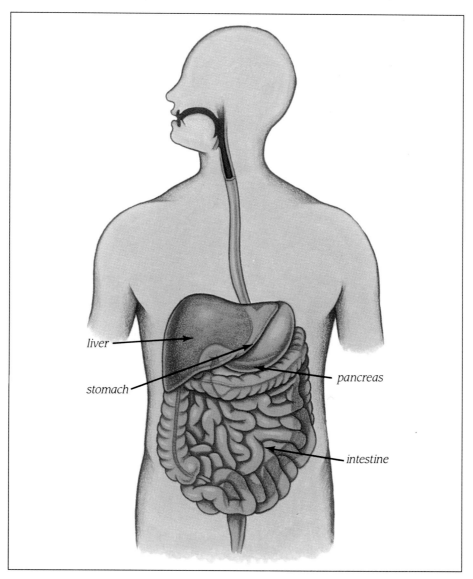

Food passes from the stomach to the intestine, where enzymes help break the nutrients down to their smallest units. The nutrients are absorbed from the intestine into the blood, which carries them to the liver. Blood from the liver returns to the heart to be pumped through the rest of the body.

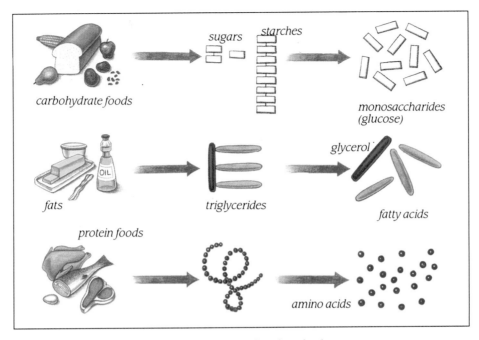

Nutrients are broken down before they can be absorbed.

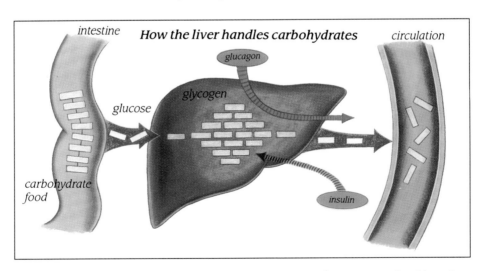

Carbohydrate foods are absorbed from the intestine as the monosaccharide unit, glucose. In the liver, insulin promotes conversion to glycogen for storage, while glucagon promotes conversion back to glucose for release into circulation.

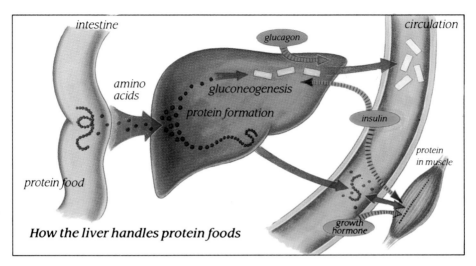

How the liver handles protein foods

Protein foods are absorbed from the intestine as amino acids. In the liver, some are built into new proteins, and some are converted by gluconeogenesis into glucose. Insulin and growth hormone both promote build-up of protein in muscle. Insulin slows gluconeogenesis while glucagon promotes it.

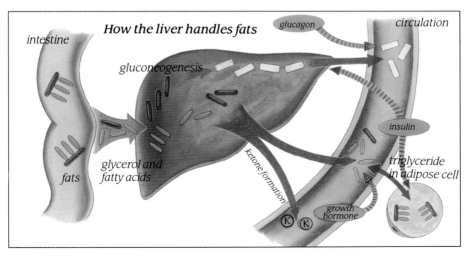

How the liver handles fats

Fats are absorbed from the intestine as glycerol and fatty acids. Some of the glycerol is converted by gluconeogenesis to glucose. Some of the fatty acids are converted to ketones. Insulin slows gluconeogenesis, while glucagon promotes it. Insulin promotes storage of triglyceride in adipose cells, while growth hormone promotes release of stored fat.

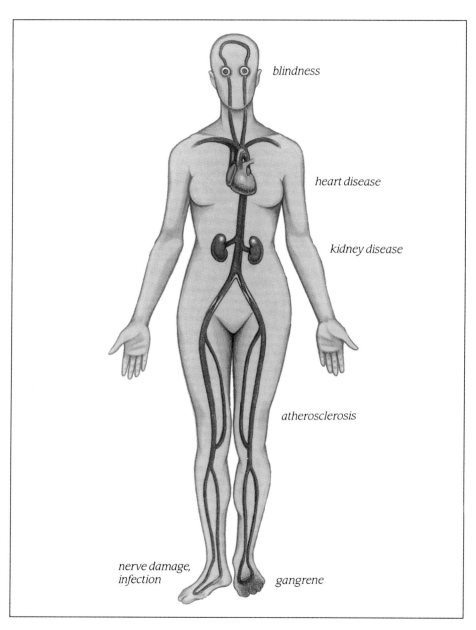

blindness

heart disease

kidney disease

atherosclerosis

nerve damage, infection

gangrene

The damage from diabetes.

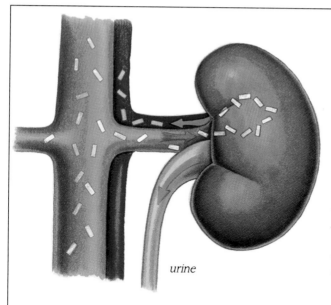

urine

Normally, there is no glucose in urine because the kidney keeps all of it in the body.

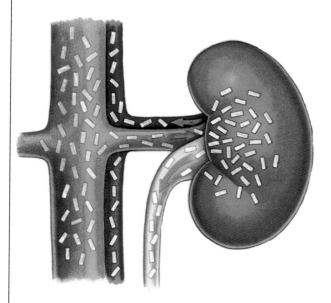

In diabetes, there may be so much glucose in the blood that the kidney can't hold all of it. Then some glucose spills out into the urine, drawing a large amount of water out with it.

Type I diabetes

- About 10 percent of all cases of diabetes
- Appears mostly in children and young adults
- Males and females, whites and blacks affected about equally
- Usually develops quickly
- No insulin produced – patients must take insulin

Type II diabetes

- Almost 90 percent of all cases of diabetes
- Appears mostly in obese older people
- Females and blacks affected more often
- Usually develops slowly
- Some insulin produced – most patients don't need to take insulin

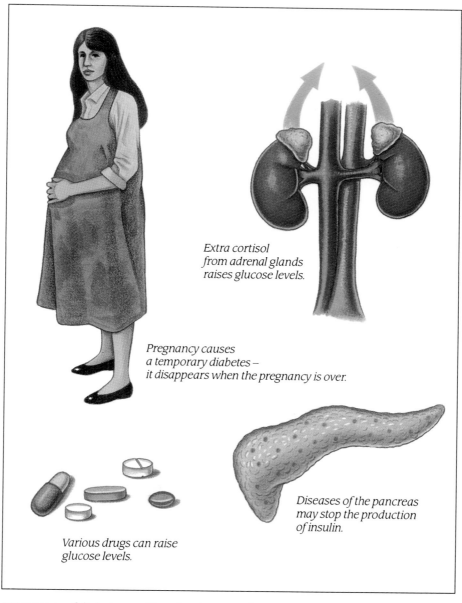

Extra cortisol
from adrenal glands
raises glucose levels.

Pregnancy causes
a temporary diabetes –
it disappears when the pregnancy is over.

Diseases of the pancreas
may stop the production
of insulin.

Various drugs can raise
glucose levels.

Most cases of diabetes are Type I or Type II. There are also some less common causes.

The Treatment of Diabetes

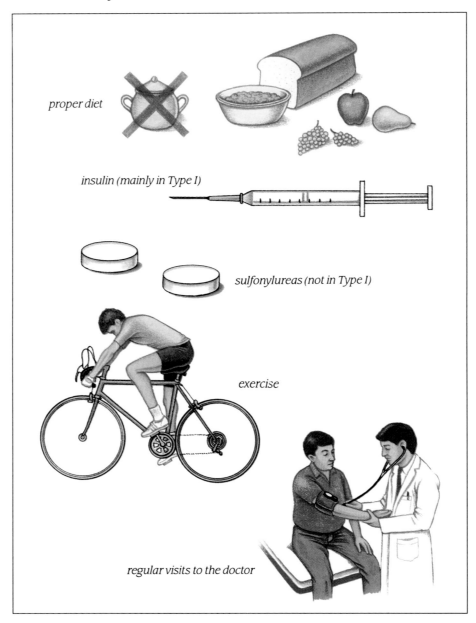

proper diet

insulin (mainly in Type I)

sulfonylureas (not in Type I)

exercise

regular visits to the doctor

 # 5: OTHER TYPES OF DIABETES

A number of other physical conditions can cause problems with glucose metabolism. But such cases are rare. In each of these conditions, people who do not have Type I or Type II diabetes still have hyperglycemia.

PREGNANCY
Between 1 and 2 percent of all pregnant women develop diabetes for the first time during the pregnancy. This group is different from women who had Type I or Type II diabetes and then became pregnant. Diabetes that appears during pregnancy goes away by itself after the pregnancy is over, but it may return if the woman becomes pregnant again. These women are also more likely than other women to develop Type II diabetes later on.

It is very important to control diabetes during pregnancy. Any kind of diabetes can make the pregnancy more difficult, and it can cause harm to both the mother and the baby. Women who develop diabetes during pregnancy must watch for any sign that the disease is coming back in the years after their babies are born.

SECONDARY DIABETES

Unlike Type I and Type II diabetes, some cases of diabetes are caused by other conditions. In many cases, the diabetes will go away if the cause of the problem is corrected.

Since insulin is made in the pancreas, any condition that affects the pancreas can cause diabetes. For example, insulin production may slow down or even stop because of an injury to the pancreas, or because of pancreas disease caused by drinking too much alcohol. And of course, insulin won't be made at all if the pancreas must be removed by surgery (often because a tumor is growing inside it).

The adrenal* glands make several hormones, including one called cortisol*. Cortisol raises glucose levels in the blood. There are a number of diseases of the adrenal glands in which large amounts of cortisol are released into the blood. Also, some people take drugs that have the same effects as cortisol. Whenever there is a large amount of cortisol or a drug that acts like cortisol in the body, hyperglycemia can occur.

Other drugs can also disturb glucose metabolism. These include different kinds of hormone-drugs, and drugs used in treating cancer, high blood pressure, and mental problems. Hyperglycemia is not a very common side effect of drugs, but it can happen.

In certain genetic disorders, people may be born with several different problems, including diabetes. It is often difficult or even impossible to correct these kinds of conditions.

DIABETES MAY APPEAR LATER

There are many people who don't have diabetes now, but are more likely than other people to develop diabetes in the future. For example, a number of people who are quite healthy will get abnormal results if they take a certain type of laboratory test that is used in diagnosing diabetes (see Chapter Six). Some – but not all – of these people will develop Type I or Type II diabetes later on. Some of those who don't become diabetics can develop atherosclerosis in the larger blood vessels, but they do not get the special kind of small-vessel damage that occurs only in people with real diabetes.

Also, there are people who are more likely than others to develop diabetes in the future simply because they belong to groups in which diabetes is more common. We have already learned about some of these groups: women who developed diabetes during pregnancy, obese people, and members of certain racial groups.

THE "OPPOSITE" OF DIABETES

Hypoglycemia* means "low levels of glucose in the blood." Since glucose is normally the main fuel for the brain, a sudden drop in glucose levels can make a person feel sick and nervous. If the blood glucose level drops very low, a person may become unconscious. This condition is sometimes caused by a tumor in the Islets of Langerhans in the pancreas. The tumor produces insulin even when the blood glucose level is already low (usually, when the person doesn't eat anything for a while), and that pushes the glucose level even lower. Some children become hypoglycemic when they don't eat, even if they produce insulin normally. Other people become

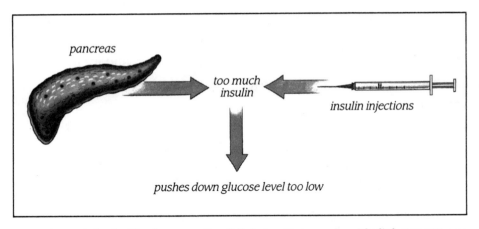

pancreas

too much insulin

insulin injections

pushes down glucose level too low

Hypoglycemia looks like the opposite of diabetes. But people with diabetes can cause hypoglycemia by injecting too much insulin.

hypoglycemic right after they eat. Most of these people have had stomach surgery at some time in the past. Now, when they eat, food enters the intestine very quickly, glucose is absorbed into the blood very quickly, and the pancreas has to produce insulin very quickly. Sometimes, so much insulin is made that it pushes the blood glucose level down below normal. These people must avoid eating too much sugar or starch at any one time, because that can trigger a sudden surge of insulin from the pancreas.

This type of hypoglycemia, which occurs as a reaction to a meal, is rarely found in people who have *not* had stomach surgery – but for some reason, many people who have not had any surgery *think* they have this condition.

Hypoglycemia looks a little like the opposite of diabetes – there is too much insulin at work instead of too little, and the blood glucose level is too low instead of too high. But diabetics can also become hypoglycemic, if they take too much insulin by injection or if they don't eat enough while taking insulin (see Chapter Seven).

Because there are many different kinds of diabetes, there may be many different signs of the disease. In the next chapter, we will see how doctors can demonstrate that a person has diabetes.

 # 6: DIAGNOSING DIABETES

Diabetes has many effects on the body, but certain effects are especially common. From these clues, a doctor may suspect that a person has diabetes. Then medical tests are done to prove it.

SYMPTOMS OF DIABETES

The most common symptoms are polydypsia* (frequent drinking because of unusually great thirst) and polyuria* (production of an unusually large amount of urine). Both of these symptoms are caused by hyperglycemia. When there is a very high concentration of any substance in the blood, the brain causes the person to feel thirsty.

In diabetes, the glucose concentration is often high. The diabetic feels thirsty and drinks some water, and that reduces the glucose concentration. But there is still a lot of glucose in the blood. Then, as the blood passes through the kidneys, a load of glucose spills out into the urine and draws a large amount of water out with it. That loss of water again raises the concentration of substances in the blood, and that again causes thirst. Since diabetes tends to keep raising the glucose levels, polydypsia and polyuria keep occurring.

Sometimes, people go to a doctor for another problem, without knowing that they have diabetes. But something will make the doctor suspect diabetes. For example, if a person has frequent infections, the doctor may think about the fact that germs grow quickly in areas where the glucose level is high and the blood circulation is poor – conditions that occur in diabetes. Or a person may have lost all feeling in the foot or some other part of the body, and the doctor will think about how diabetes can damage the nerves.

In Type I diabetes, the breakdown of fat and protein (caused by the lack of insulin) often leads to a loss of weight even though the person is eating a lot. People with Type I disease, unlike most of the people who get Type II disease, are often underweight. Feeling hungry is common in both conditions.

Type I diabetes often develops quickly. In some cases, the person may have symptoms or may feel sick for only a day or two, and then the condition becomes rapidly worse. In very bad cases, the person becomes comatose* (unconscious) because of severe acidosis, and diabetes is not diagnosed until the person has been brought to the hospital.

Type II diabetes usually develops more slowly, with symptoms of polydypsia and polyuria. The condition may not even be noticed, especially when it occurs in very old people who are less aware of what is happening to their bodies.

Other forms of diabetes are

often found accidentally, by a laboratory test that measures the amount of glucose in the urine or blood.

LABORATORY TESTS

As soon as the doctor suspects that a person has diabetes, the next step is to confirm it – to prove that the person does or does not have diabetes. There are several tests that can confirm the diagnosis, and all of them work by measuring glucose levels.

The simplest kind of test uses a little plastic stick made with special chemicals that change color when the stick is dipped into a liquid, according to how much glucose is present in the liquid. Some of these "dipsticks" are made for testing urine, and some are made for testing blood.

MEASURING GLUCOSE IN THE URINE

Normally, there is no glucose at all in urine, because the kidneys are always working to keep as much glucose as possible in the body. Even when there is a little too much glucose in the blood, the kidneys are able to keep all of it in the body. But in diabetes, there may be so much glucose in the blood that the kidneys just can't hold on to all of it. Whatever the kidneys can't keep inside the body will come out into the urine, and the dipstick test will show that. The same kind of test can be done with a chemical tablet instead of a dipstick.

Some people have glucose in the urine even though they don't have diabetes. That is caused by a problem in the kidneys – if the kidneys can't hold on to glucose, it will spill out into the urine even though the amount of glucose in the blood is normal. The way to tell if that is happening is by testing the blood.

MEASURING GLUCOSE IN THE BLOOD

Dipsticks can show how much

glucose is in a drop of blood. This kind of test is fairly accurate – but to get a very precise measurement, a sample of blood must be analyzed in a medical laboratory. Measurements can be made from a sample of blood that is taken randomly (at any time); or from a sample taken after a person has fasted (not eaten anything) overnight; or from samples taken after a person has fasted and then eaten a certain amount of glucose.

The first kind of test, using blood taken at any time, is the simplest, since there is no preparation necessary. In fact, it is often done routinely, when people have any kind of medical examination. Sometimes, that is how diabetes is discovered. The glucose level is somewhat higher right after a meal than it will be a few hours later, after insulin has had time to take the glucose that was absorbed from the food and get it into the cells or converted to glycogen or fat

for storage. But in Type I diabetics who are not yet under treatment, the glucose level is usually at least three times higher than normal. In Type II diabetics, the glucose level may not be that high – and the doctor might not be sure whether it is high because the sample was taken right after the person ate or because the person has diabetes. Then a more definite kind of test is needed.

When the blood sample is taken after the person has fasted overnight, the doctor knows that the glucose level is not being affected by a recent meal. If it is high, it is not normal.

THE GLUCOSE TOLERANCE TEST

The most definite test is called the Glucose Tolerance Test, which shows how well the body "tolerates" (responds to) a meal of glucose. After the person fasts overnight, a blood sample is taken to measure the fasting level of glucose. Then the

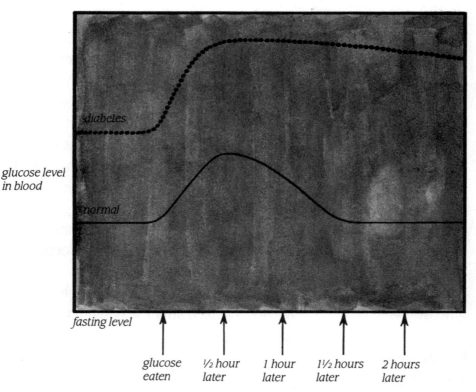

glucose level
in blood

diabetes

normal

fasting level

glucose
eaten

½ hour
later

1 hour
later

1½ hours
later

2 hours
later

On the Glucose Tolerance Test, the person with diabetes has a high fasting level of glucose, and the level rises higher and stays higher than in a healthy person.

person eats a meal that contains a precise amount of glucose, and blood samples are taken and tested every half-hour for the next two hours. In a nondiabetic person, the fasting level is normal, and the measurements taken over the next two hours show that the glucose level in the blood rises only a certain amount after the meal and then falls back quickly toward normal. But in a person with diabetes, the fasting level is usually high, and the glucose level rises higher and stays high for a longer time than in the nondiabetic. As we learned in

Chapter Five, there are people who do not have diabetes but do have abnormal results on this test. Usually, their glucose levels are somewhere between normal levels and the levels seen in people with diabetes.

Since the glucose tolerance test requires overnight fasting and several samples of blood, many doctors first try random or fasting measurements when they suspect that a person has diabetes. If those tests are normal, there is no need to do the glucose tolerance test. If those tests are not normal, the glucose tolerance test is the best way to prove that the person does or doesn't have diabetes. However, the test does not show whether diabetes is Type I, Type II, or some other type. The doctor must use all the information gathered from talking to the person, from a careful physical examination, and from other laboratory tests to find out what type of diabetes the person has and whether it is being caused by some other condition.

Proper treatment depends on knowing what type of diabetes a person has, as we will see in the next chapter.

7: TREATING DIABETES

Most experts think that a lot of the damage caused by diabetes can be prevented by keeping the disease under control. In any kind of diabetes, that means keeping blood glucose levels as steady and as close to normal as possible. In cases of diabetes caused by another condition, the other condition must be corrected if that is possible.

Daily treatment of diabetes consists of proper diet and exercise, insulin or other drugs (for some patients), and doing tests at home to see if treatment is keeping the glucose level under control. And of course, any patient with diabetes must see his or her doctor regularly.

Although diabetes is a serious condition, patients can do a lot for themselves in treating it – more than patients with many other kinds of disorders can do for themselves.

44

DIET AND EXERCISE

Diabetics do not need any special foods. But they must take special care in planning what and when they eat. Eating too much will just make a person gain weight. Eating foods that contain lots of sugar will raise the blood glucose level. Eating too little or at long intervals while taking insulin will let the glucose level fall too low. A proper diet will supply all the nutrients the body needs while keeping the glucose level steady and the body weight normal.

Obese patients – which means the majority of those with Type II diabetes – should try to lose weight. However, the younger people who get Type I diabetes are often underweight. They may have to gain to reach a normal body weight. If they are still growing, their diets must supply even more calories to help them maintain normal weight while allowing for growth.

For both groups, the majority of the calories in food should come from carbohydrates (starches, not sugars!), and the rest should come about equally from proteins and fats. All or most of the fat should come from plant foods like nuts and seeds, with as little animal fat as possible. Each person's diet must be designed according to the type of diabetes; the person's age, general health, and daily activities; and the schedule of insulin therapy (for those patients who must take insulin).

Exercise is also a very important part of treatment. It helps in building and strengthening the body, and it is very good for the heart.

In other words, the diabetic person should follow the same program of sensible diet and exercise that a nondiabetic person would follow to stay healthy. But for the diabetic person, it is even more important. No treatment plan

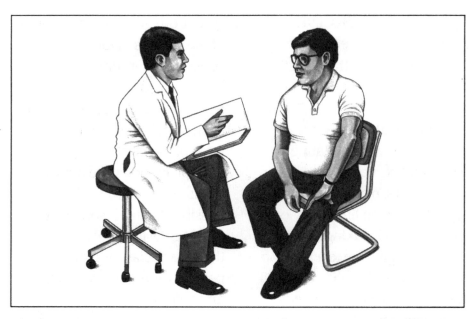

The doctor or a dietician must plan a proper diet that is made especially for each patient. The doctor must also plan drug treatment in diabetics who need insulin or sulfonylurea drugs.

for diabetes will work unless the person stays on a good diet. In many cases of Type II diabetes, that is the only treatment needed. For people who have always eaten foods that are loaded with sugar and animal fat, it may take a little time to get used to a good diet. But it is very important to try – because the very same diet that helps in treating diabetes is also good for preventing many kinds of heart disease and cancer.

The family can help a lot, by encouraging the diabetic patient to stay on a proper diet, and by helping the patient watch for any signs of problems that may arise.

INSULIN
Since people with Type I diabetes do not produce any

insulin, they must take it by injection. Insulin, like all hormones, is a protein, and that is why it must be taken by injection. If it were taken by mouth, the body would just break it down before absorbing it – and it would no longer be insulin, but just a set of amino acids.

In severe cases of Type II diabetes, a proper diet may not be enough. These patients must also take insulin or other drugs to help keep their glucose levels under control. But in many cases of Type II diabetes, insulin doesn't even work, because the liver keeps making new glucose at a very fast rate.

Most diabetics take insulin that is made from the pancreas of pigs or cattle. Scientists have recently learned how to make human insulin in the laboratory, and a growing number of patients are now using this type of insulin, even though it costs a little more than pork or beef insulin.

Insulin can be prepared so that it will work very quickly but only for a short time, or more slowly over a longer time. The doctor must choose the right kind of insulin to use, the right dose, and the right schedule for taking it. Like diet, insulin treatment must be planned specially for each patient.

Patients who need insulin must learn how to inject it so that they can take it at home. Some patients are not able to give themselves injections, and then a family member must help.

DRUGS TAKEN BY MOUTH

No one likes to take injections, so doctors and scientists have looked for drugs that would work like insulin, but could be taken by mouth. They found a group of chemical compounds called sulfonylureas*. These drugs may work by increasing the amount of insulin coming from the beta-cells in the pancreas. They may also slow down the process of

47

gluconeogenesis in the liver, and improve the cells' responses to the presence of insulin, such as by increasing the number of insulin receptors on the cell surfaces. But sulfonylurea drugs do not work unless the pancreas is still producing some insulin. Therefore, they cannot be used in Type I diabetics, who have no insulin production at all.

Like all drugs, the sulfonylureas can cause serious side effects, and doctors do not like to use them unless they are really needed. They can help in those cases of Type II diabetes where diet alone is not enough. Pregnant women should not take these drugs, no matter what type of diabetes they have.

TESTS DONE AT HOME

Most people with diabetes do tests in their own homes to see how well their glucose levels are being controlled. They can use a dipstick or a chemical tablet to see if there is glucose in the urine. Some patients also test their own blood, making a small cut on the finger with a clean, sharp point to get a drop of blood. Most patients who test their own blood use a dipstick, which can show if there is any big change in the glucose level. A number of diabetic patients are now using a machine at home to read the results from the dipstick. The machine gives a precise measurement, just like a laboratory test.

People with Type I diabetes also have to test for ketones in the urine. A special kind of chemical tablet placed in the urine shows if ketones are present, which would mean that stored fat is being released and broken down too fast. When that happens, the dose of insulin must be increased; otherwise, acidosis can develop as ketones build up in the body.

Any kind of sickness or injury can upset glucose metabolism in diabetics. That is why testing is very important even for

Many patients with diabetes use dipsticks to see how much glucose is in the urine. The chemicals on the dipstick change color according to the level of glucose in the urine. Some diabetics also test their blood to measure the glucose level.

people who stay on a good diet, get regular exercise, and take insulin or sulfonylurea drugs just the way their doctors have ordered.

EMERGENCIES

Most emergencies in diabetes are related to very large changes in blood glucose levels – extreme hyperglycemia or hypoglycemia.

Fortunately, these conditions don't develop very often, because patients watch their glucose levels at home and correct any changes before they get too large.

Acidosis, from a build-up of ketones, can develop if a person with Type I diabetes is not taking enough insulin. In severe acidosis, the patient will be in a coma, with very high levels of glucose, fatty acids, and ketones in the blood. The patient has probably also lost a great deal of water in the urine while the glucose level was rising and the acidosis was developing. In the hospital, doctors must keep injecting insulin and replacing the fluid that was lost. It takes hours to correct all these problems. Without treatment, acidosis can lead to death.

A person with Type I diabetes can also develop hypoglycemia – low glucose levels – usually from eating too little or taking too much insulin. At first,
hypoglycemia can just make a person feel hungry and maybe a little nervous. Later, as the condition gets worse, the person may feel cold and sweaty, and even more nervous. Some patients become confused, angry, or even violent. In a few cases, the blood glucose level falls so low that the person becomes unconscious.

All of these conditions develop because the brain is not getting the fuel it needs. Normally, the brain uses glucose for fuel, and gluconeogenesis supplies enough glucose for the brain even when there is no more glycogen to convert to glucose. Then, as stored fat starts to be released and broken down, the brain can also use ketones for fuel. But insulin slows down gluconeogenesis and ketone production in the liver. Therefore, too much insulin not only takes too much glucose out of the blood, it also stops the formation of glucose and ketones – and then the brain has neither glucose nor ketones, which are the only fuels it can use.

Doctors can treat hypoglycemia by giving glucose until the level in the blood comes back up to normal. But in many homes, the parents of children taking insulin for Type I diabetes keep some glucagon ready to inject in case of hypoglycemia caused by taking too much insulin. Glucagon, the hormone from the alpha-cells of the pancreas, acts in the opposite way from insulin, raising blood glucose levels.

People with Type II diabetes rarely develop acidosis, and only those who take insulin can develop hypoglycemia. But they can still become severely hyperglycemic – and if the level of glucose in the blood is high enough, that alone can cause coma or death. Doctors treat this condition by giving insulin to reduce the glucose level, and fluids to replace what was lost in the urine.

GOING INTO THE HOSPITAL

The best way for diabetics to avoid having to go into the hospital is by following a proper diet, taking insulin or other drugs as their doctors have prescribed, and testing their glucose levels at home. In most cases, that is enough. Emergencies are rare, because diabetics soon learn to deal with changes in glucose levels before bad problems develop.

Diabetic patients might also have to go into the hospital if damage to the blood vessels causes serious problems like gangrene in the feet, kidney disease, or heart disease. But again, the best way to avoid that is by keeping the disease under control with a program of careful diet and exercise.

Can we do anything more to deal with diabetes?

8: THE OUTLOOK FOR DIABETES

Although there is still no cure for diabetes, scientists are always looking for new and better ways to treat it. For example, human insulin can now be manufactured in the laboratory, as we learned. This type of insulin causes fewer problems than beef or pork insulin, so more and more patients are using it.

Some patients who must take insulin now carry a little pump with them. The device pumps insulin into the body through a tube that goes under the skin. Although this system avoids the need for the patient to take several injections during the day, there are still problems with it, such as infections developing at the place where the tube goes into the skin. Also, the tube must be replaced and repositioned regularly, which is done through a large needle.

Scientists are now developing

a pump that can be implanted inside the body. If that were controlled by a device that could automatically measure blood glucose levels, it would release insulin gradually throughout the day, in response to changes in the glucose level – just as the pancreas releases insulin in nondiabetic people.

Another way in which scientists are trying to make the control of insulin closer to normal is by transplanting healthy Islet cells (with insulin-producing beta-cells) into the pancreas in diabetic patients. This is still an experimental procedure, but many scientists expect that it will be used widely in the future.

Doctors have also learned how to treat some of the damage caused by diabetes. They can use lasers* to repair tiny blood vessels in the eye. And they can transplant a healthy kidney into a diabetic whose kidneys have stopped working.

BUT WHAT ABOUT PREVENTION?

Although treatment is improving, more and more people are getting diabetes. One reason is that people are living longer – long enough to develop Type II diabetes, the most common type in this country. But Type II diabetes doesn't happen just because a person grows older, or else everyone would have it after a certain age. Some people are more likely than others to get Type II diabetes, but they can still do a lot to prevent it – mainly by following a proper diet. Unfortunately, most Americans still eat far too much sugar and fat. That is why so many people are obese, and why many of them will develop Type II diabetes. Doctors can't prevent it. Only people themselves can, by eating and living in an intelligent way.

We don't know how to prevent Type I diabetes from happening. But with any type of diabetes,

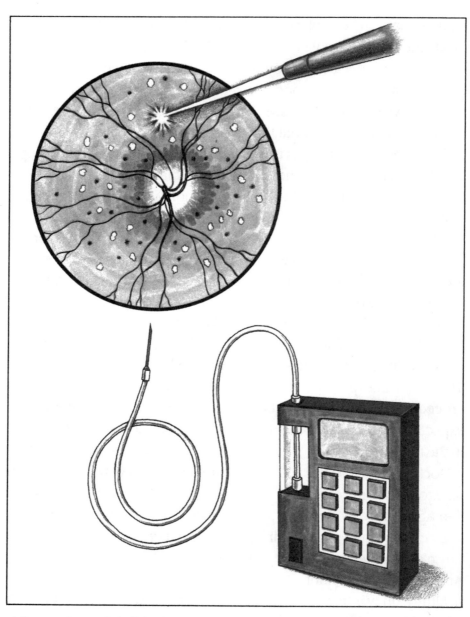

Advances in treating diabetes include repair of little blood vessels at the back of the eye, using lasers; and the insulin pump.

keeping body weight and blood glucose levels as close to normal as possible can prevent emergency conditions like hypoglycemia and hyperglycemia; that also reduces the chance of developing problems caused by damage to blood vessels. Doctors and scientists may someday find better treatments. In the meantime, diabetics can usually keep the condition under control by their own efforts.

GLOSSARY

Acidosis *(a-si-DOH-sis)*. A very serious change in the body's chemical balance, caused by a build-up of acids. In diabetes, it is usually a build-up of ketones, which are produced in the liver from fatty acids. Doctors call this condition ketoacidosis *(KEE-toh-a-si-DOH-sis)*.

Adipose *(ADD-i-pose)*. Tissue made up of cells that are designed to store fat around the body. Fats are stored in a form called triglycerides.

Adrenal glands *(a-DREE-nul)*. Two glands found on top of the kidneys. They make a number of different hormones, including cortisol.

Amino acid *(a-MEE-no)*. Any one of a group of twenty-one compounds that come from protein foods. They can be linked together in any number of different combinations to form new proteins for the body.

Atherosclerosis *(ATH-er-o-skle-RO-sis)*. A disease in which fatty deposits form inside blood vessels, which are then hardened by calcium. These deposits reduce the amount of blood that can flow through the vessel and force the heart to work harder.

Carbohydrate *(KAR-bo-HI-drate)*. One of the groups of nutrients in food. Carbohydrates are made of units called saccharides. The two main types of carbohydrate are sugars and starches.

Comatose *(KO-ma-tose)*. In a coma – that is, unconscious. In diabetes, people can become comatose from acidosis or severe hyperglycemia or hypoglycemia, which are all emergencies.

Cortisol *(KOR-ti-sawl)*. One of the hormones made by the adrenal glands. Cortisol has many effects on the body, including the ability to raise the level of glucose in the blood during times of stress, such as sickness or injury.

Dehydrated *(DEE-hi-dray-ted)*. Suffering from a large loss of water from the body. In diabetes, dehydration happens when there is too much glucose in the blood for the kidney to hold. The excess glucose spills out into the urine and draws a large amount of water out with it.

Enzyme *(EN-zime)*. A type of protein that promotes chemical reactions. Many enzymes are used in digesting food. These reactions break the nutrients into their smallest units so that they can be absorbed.

Fatty acid *(FAT-tee)*. A chain of carbon atoms with hydrogen atoms attached to it. Three long chains are linked to glycerol to form a triglyceride (fat). By themselves, fatty acids can be used as fuel for most parts of the body except the brain.

Gangrene *(GANG-reen)*. The death of tissue from lack of blood. In diabetes, gangrene most often occurs in the feet because of damage to blood vessels. Dead tissue must be removed by surgery, and that often means the whole foot must be amputated.

Glucagon *(GLOO-ka-gon)*. A hormone from the alpha-cells of the Islets of Langerhans in the pancreas. Glucagon raises the level of glucose in the blood – the opposite of what insulin does.

Gluconeogenesis *(GLOO-ko-nee-o-JEN-a-sis)*. The production of new glucose using glycerol from fat, and certain amino acids from proteins. This process takes place in the liver. Glucagon promotes gluconeogenesis, while insulin opposes it.

Glucose *(GLOO-kose)*. The monosaccharide that is finally formed from the breakdown of all carbohydrates. It is the best fuel for most of the body cells. Many of the problems in diabetes are caused by the fact that the glucose level in the blood is not controlled.

Glycerol *(GLISS-er-awl)*. A molecule that links three long fatty acid chains to form a triglyceride. When triglycerides break down, glycerol can be converted into new glucose in the liver (gluconeogenesis), while excess glucose can be converted to glycerol to form more triglyceride for storage in adipose cells.

Glycogen *(GLY-ko-jen)*. A changed form of glucose that is stored in the liver and muscles. As glucose in the blood is used for fuel, it is replaced by the conversion of glycogen back to glucose. When the supply of glycogen has gone down, the body starts using fatty acids for fuel.

Hormone *(HOR-mone)*. A type of protein that controls the way different organs and tissues in the body do their jobs. Insulin, glucagon, and cortisol are just three of many different hormones that the body uses.

Hyperglycemia *(HI-per-gly-SEE-mee-a)*. Too much glucose in the blood. This is the most common problem in diabetes, and it usually occurs because there is not enough insulin.

Hypoglycemia *(HI-po-gly-SEE-mee-a)*. Too little glucose in the blood. Some people have this condition because they produce too much of their own insulin. In diabetes, it usually occurs when people inject too much insulin.

Insulin *(IN-suh-lin)*. A hormone made by the beta-cells of the Islets of Langerhans in the pancreas. Insulin lowers the level of glucose in the blood – the opposite of what glucagon does. Diabetes is caused by a lack of insulin action.

Islets of Langerhans *(EYE-lets, LAHNG-er-hahnz)*. Special areas inside the pancreas that make glucagon and insulin. They were named after Paul Langerhans, a German scientist who discovered them in the nineteenth century.

Ketones *(KEE-tones)*. A group of acid chemicals made in the liver from fatty acids. They are another form of fuel, especially used by the muscles. When too much fatty acid is released from the breakdown of triglycerides, ketones are made faster than they can be used. Then they pile up in the body, causing acidosis.

Laser *(LAY-zer)*. A machine that makes a special kind of light-beam that can cut through objects like a knife. Lasers are sometimes used in surgery. They can be used to repair small blood vessels in the eye damaged by diabetes.

Metabolism *(muh-TAB-o-lizz-em)*. All the processes that are involved with absorbing and using the nutrients in food. There are separate metabolic *(MET-a-BAHL-ick)* processes for carbohydrates, proteins, and fats, and all of them can be upset by diabetes.

Pancreas *(PANK-re-us)*. An organ located just below the stomach. Most of the tissue of the pancreas is involved with producing different enzymes that enter the intestine to help digest all the different nutrients from food. Inside the pancreas are the Islets of Langerhans.

Polydypsia *(PAH-lee-DIP-see-a)*. Excessive thirst. It is caused by a high concentration of glucose in the blood and the loss of large amounts of water in the urine. Polydypsia occurs along with polyuria, and these are the most common symptoms of diabetes.

Polyuria *(PAH-lee-YOOR-ee-a)*. Excessive urination. It is caused by excess glucose spilling out into the urine, drawing a large amount of water out with it. Polyuria can lead to dehydration.

Protein *(PRO-teen)*. The material used to build almost every kind of structure in the body, including cells, enzymes, and hormones. Proteins are made up of chains of amino acids in different combinations. Protein from food must be broken down to its amino acids so that they can be absorbed and then built into new proteins that the body can use.

Receptor *(ree-SEP-ter)*. A special area on the surface of cells, designed to link with a particular type of molecule. Insulin must bind to insulin receptors before it can start doing its jobs, such as getting glucose inside the cell for use as fuel.

Saccharide *(SACK-a-ride)*. The basic unit of all carbohydrates. The word saccharide is rarely used by itself. Instead, sugars are called monosaccharides if they consist of just one unit, or disaccharides if they consist of two units, while starches are called polysaccharides because they consist of long chains with many units.

Sulfonylurea *(sull-FAH-nill-yoo-REE-a)*. A type of drug that reduces the level of glucose in the blood, possibly by causing the beta-cells in the Islets of Langerhans to release more insulin, or by improving the cells' response to insulin. These drugs can be used in Type II diabetes, but not in Type I, because they work only if the body is still producing some insulin.

Triglyceride *(try-GLISS-a-ride).* The form of fat that is stored in adipose tissue around the body. It is made up of three long chains of fatty acid linked by glycerol.

INDEX

ABOUT THE AUTHOR

Steven Tiger is a graduate of Brooklyn College and the Physician Assistant Program of Touro College, New York City. Formerly in clinical practice as a physician assistant, he has been editing and writing for numerous medical journals and is also a guest lecturer in medical physiology at the Physician Assistant Program, The Brooklyn Hospital / Long Island University. He is the author of *Arthritis* and *Heart Disease* in the Understanding Disease series.